Widows Sons

Outlaw Bikers or Masonic Ambassadors

Widows Sons
Outlaw Bikers or Masonic Ambassadors

Wayne Pendragon Owens

Pendragon Press

First published in 2022

By Pendragon Press

ISBN 9798839101005

Pendragon Press

https://pendragonpress.uk

Contents

Introduction.

2018 marked the twentieth anniversary of the creation of the Widows Sons, with 2019 marking the fifteenth anniversary of the Widows Sons starting in the UK.

We are fully recognised, and approved by the United Grand Lodge of England, even featuring prominently on the main page of their website. We have had articles about us in multiple issues of "The Square Magazine", as well as being often mentioned in "Freemasonry Today", and were the main part of the third episode of Sky's five-part documentary series "Inside the Freemasons".

Even so, until recently, not many brethren had heard of us, or knew what it is we do, they may have just seen us an Outlaw biker gang. To be fair we do have some scary looking members.

To help spread word about us, especially in the Province of North Wales, I wrote a talk originally called "Widows Sons – Brotherhood Squared" which I would give at Lodge meetings as a brief introduction of where we came from, who we are, and what we do.

Over time this talk grew and changed, even appearing in The Square Magazine in a cut down version. Eventually it became "Widows Sons – Outlaw Bikers or Masonic Ambassadors."

Recently I saw someone on Twitter post: -

> "JUST SEEN SOMEONE FROM THE WIDOWS SONS WALKING AROUND NEAR THE CASTLE. AM I THE ONLY ONE WHO THINKS THE MOTORCYCLE GANG LOOK ISN'T VERY COMING OF FREEMASONRY? CALL ME OLD FASHIONED BUT LEATHER JACKETS WITH MASSIVE PATCHES LOOK TERRIBLE."

Which then led into several conversations about who or what the Widows Sons are. I therefore, decide to convert my lecture into some form of book, so that more people could learn about us and decide for themselves if we are Outlaw Bikers or Masonic Ambassadors.

Wayne Pendragon Owens
July 2022

Outlaw Bikers.

Outlaw motorcycle gangs are considered a national threat and a national policing priority in 17 EU Member States and six Europol partner states.

While most members of motorcycle clubs around the world are law abiding, a small percentage are not.

Styling themselves "outlaws" or "one-percenters", they wear a patch on their jackets showing a 1% sign inside a diamond shape. This means that they belong to an outlaw motorcycle gang, such as the Hells Angels, Bandidos or Outlaws.

Since 2005, there has been steady growth in the membership of such gangs worldwide. In Europe, the number of clubs has more than doubled.

Europol (2022)

Large groups of Motorcyclists, especially those wearing cuts and patches have been causing fear and concern to people all over the world since Outlaw Biker clubs first formed in the late 1940's after the end of World War two.

To give some examples: -

> ➤ In July 2008, a group of 50 bikers, who were just hanging around outside a club, caught the attention of German police in Berlin, which led to 34 of the bikers being arrested.

> ➤ In 2009, the Canadian Government introduced the first anti-gang law in Canadian legislation in response to the perceived threats of biker clubs.

> ➤ In 2013, Queensland introduced The Vicious Lawless Association Disestablishment Act, Or VLAD for short. This act saw 26 motorcycle clubs be classified at criminal organisations.

> ➤ Also in 2013, Europol, the EU's law enforcement agency put the UK on alert over Biker gangs bringing war to Britain. They raised fears that there would be a surge in violence as the "Outlaw Motorcycle Gangs" battled it out in the streets of our cities for supremacy and the control of organised crime markets.

> ➤ In 2015 South Australia, built on the VLAD act and introduced some of the strictest anti-bike laws on the planet, making it a criminal offense for any gatherings of 3 or more club members. And totally outlawing all colours, patches, or club insignias.

Widows Sons.

So, who are the Widows Sons?

Are we just a group of patch wearing "Outlaw Bikers", or if not, how can we claim to be ambassadors for freemasonry if bikers cause so much fear and concern everywhere they go?

If we go right back to the beginning of biker gangs, right back to July 1947. A large group of bikers descended on the small town of Hollister, California for a weekend of partying. This event resulted in the State Police being called out to clear out the bikers, and was later immortalised in the cult film "The Wild One" which itself has led to a tradition of outlaw biker films, which is still going strong with one of the top TV shows of the last decade being "The Sons of Anarchy"

Now fast forward 70 years to July 2017, and a large group of bikers from around the world descending on the small town of Mold, North Wales, for a weekend of partying, loud music, and I believe the Rugby club where they were camping was drunk dry two nights in a row. This weekend will not make it to film, or TV, but it did make it to several newspapers, with a dozen different articles on what a fantastic thing it was and congratulating the Freemasons for their donations to local charities.

THE WILD ONE
COLUMBIA PICTURES

So just who are the Widows Sons?

Brethren, we are informed that there are three epochs in the history of Freemasonry which particularly merit our attention, the history of the Widows Sons likewise has three notable epochs, namely, the First or Founding Chapters, the Second or International Chapters, and the Third or United Kingdom and Ireland Chapters.

The First or Founding Chapters.

It all started with one man, and his dream to form a Masonic motorcycle club. It started one rainy Sunday morning when Brother Carl Davenport woke with the words "Widows Sons" in his head, along with an image of a beautiful woman with a pale look to her face.

For several weeks he walked around with this image, and the words "Widows Sons" in his head, until one day while having an online conversation with a fellow Brother and discussing motorcycles and Masonry that the entire concept of a club including the logo came together in his head. The motorcycle club should be called the Widows Sons and they should aid and assist the widows of Masons whose faces were "pale white from the pain of their loss and the fear of their future travels alone."

In February 1998 at the Mirage Restaurant in Schiller Park, Illinois the first chapter of "The Widows Sons" was formed. In June, a second chapter of Widows Sons was formed in the Netherlands, making the Widows Sons an international organisation. 1999 saw chapters formed in Connecticut, and Florida, with requests from potential members wanting to start chapters coming in from across the United States and Europe.

Those first four chapters are still standing today.

Purpose of the Widows Sons.

> ➤ The sole founding goal and purposes of the original Widows Sons was to aid and assist widows and orphans of Master Masons.

> ➤ The second purpose of founding the Widows Sons was to promote fellowship and unity among brother Masons who ride motorcycles.

> ➤ The third purpose of the founding of the Widows Sons was to introduce Freemasonry to the world of motorcycling and to introduce the world of motorcycling to freemasonry.

The second, or the International Chapters.

2004 was a significant year for "The Widows Sons", by the start of the year Brother Davenport's motorcycle club had grown to have chapters spread across eleven states in the U.S. and five countries outside the U.S. Therefore, in February 2004, to help administrate this growing association the first two Grand Chapters were formed, quickly followed by a third a month later.

At the same time, in recognition of the groups growing international status the name was changed to "The International Widows Sons Masonic Riders Association" or "Widows Sons MRA" for short.

The third, or the United Kingdom and Ireland Chapters.

As mentioned 2004 was an incredibly significant year for the Widows Sons, it was also the year that The Widows Sons arrived in Great Britain with a Chapter formed by a group of Freeasons in the Nottinghamshire area.

The UK Chapter of the Widows Sons did make several changes, firstly they introduced their own alternative logo, and separated themselves from the Masonic Riders Association by calling themselves the Masonic Bikers Association. And most importunely they changed the goal and purposes, they would still introduce, and promote Freemasonry to the world of motorcycling, etc. But they changed the primary goal so that they would raise money for any charitable cause and not just to aid and assist the widows and orphans of Master Masons.

In February 2010 the Presidents Governing Board (PGB) was formed as the ruling body for The Widows Sons MBA, the membership is made up of the Presidents, Vice Presidents and the Past Presidents of each chapter in Great Britain. The Board meets twice a year and are in constant contact by electronic means.

In recent years the UK Widows Sons have split into two distinct groups. The Masonic Bikers Association (MBA) and the Masonic Riders Association (MRA).

Cut.

One of the main reasons we may get mistaken for Outlaw Bikers is our cuts, and patches.

Our waistcoats can be considered our regalia, to quote from the Widows Sons Vest Lecture "I now present you with a leather vest; It neither is a cut nor is it called colours. It is an emblem and a badge of a Widows Son. It is always to be worn with equal pleasure to yourself and honour to this fraternity. There is no other group of Freemasons with the eyes of the public on them more than the Widows Sons."

As you can see on the photographs on the next page, that there are a variety of patches worn on the cuts.

There are two patches which every Widows Son in the UK wear. They are the Badge of the Widows Sons Masonic Bikers Association; this badge must be worn on the left-hand breast close to the heart. And the Chapter Patch, which denotes the chapter they belong too.

The officers of the Chapter will also wear a badge depicting their role, Some of the officers of a Chapter are: - President, Vice President, Secretary, Treasurer, Charity Steward, Road Captain, Wardens, Almoner.

Founder members of a Chapter will have a "founders" patch.

We also have a road name which is given to the brother by the chapter.

There are also Rally and event Patches such as the 2017 North Wales Rally Patch, and Individuals may add additional patches as they wish.

Like the three epochs of the Widows Sons, there are likewise three iterations of the main patch.

Patch #1.

The original patch or logo is the "Widows Logo" also often fondly referred to as "Elvira" which was designed by Brother Carl Davenport. The idea was that the Widow would be a little bit edgy, and thus it may help to attract those men who may not otherwise be attracted to the traditional idea of suit and tie masonry.

It is used by the founding chapters, as well as a few of the more recent chapters. As you can see it is a simplistic design, being just the image of a crouching woman with the words Widows Sons.

Patch #2.

In May 2004, to appease concerns regarding the lack of "Masonic relevance" of the original "Widows Logo", an alternative version was introduced. This is known as the "Modern Logo" or "Winged Logo"

The stone triangle or pyramid represents the three degrees in craft Masonry. The All-Seeing-Eye within the pyramid represents the watchfulness of the Great Architect of the Universe. It reminds us that we are always being watched or observed, and our actions recorded.

Within the points of the triangle are the symbols representing the three principal officer jewels: the Square, Plumb, and Level. These working tools are also representative of the 3 Lesser Lights and their Masonic interpretations.

The Rising Sun at the apex of the pyramid is representative of the fact that there are Masonic Lodges in all points of the globe. It can truly be said that "the sun never sets on Freemasonry".

The sun also represents the Worshipful Master of each Lodge, so the sun is positioned above the pinnacle of the pyramid and above the Square, or Master's Jewel.

The wings represent personal freedom and liberty which is an ideal Freemasons have embraced since the beginnings of our ancient and noble fraternity. Wings are also a symbol which is often embraced by those who enjoy motorcycling and are used on many logo's and badges.

The words "Meet on the level & Part upon the square" were added to remind our non-riding brethren that the Widows Sons are Masons above all, and we should be greeted and treated as such.

Now that all sounds rather impressive, and an exceptionally good reason to make the patch more symbolically masonic.

I am now going to hammer another nail into the coffin of the Widows Sons being tough outlaw bikers and admit that whilst what I have just written is the accepted reason for the new patch, and it is what you will find listed on Widows Sons Websites, Histories, and pamphlets. It is not the main reason for the change.

I heard from the co-founder of the Widows Sons that the real reason for the change was that the then President of the Northern Jurisdiction, and designer of the new patch, begged for the change because his wife hated the original patch, and other bikers made fun of him while he was out riding, and more importantly his wife REALLY hated the original patch. Proving, even leather clad, tough bikers must listen to "her indoors"

Patch #3.

This is the patch designed for the Widows Sons UK.

The Square and Compasses being the single most universally identifiable symbol of Freemasonry, are placed predominantly on the patch to signify we are Freemasons above all else.

Just under the Square and Compasses is the Volume of the Sacred Law. Giving us representation of the three great, though emblematical lights in Freemasonry. The Sacred Writings are to govern our faith, the Square to regulate our actions, and the Compasses to keep us in due bounds with all mankind, particularly our brethren in Freemasonry

The two great pillars represent the Law of the Land, and the Law of God, and remind us that only by balancing the Materialistic and Spiritual pursuits will we find stability.

Surrounding the design are sprigs of acacia, symbolising the immortality of the soul, being intended to remind us, by its evergreen and unchanging nature, of that better and spiritual part within us, which, as an emanation from the Great Architect of the Universe, can never die.

Combined, the Patch has the three Greater lights representing the Entered Apprentice degree, the two pillars representing the Fellowcraft, and the sprig of acacia representing the Master Mason, illustrating the path a person needs to take to become a Master Mason, and thus be entitled to wear this patch.

Remember while we may wear identifying patches or regalia, it should be noted that the Widows Sons are not a gang, MC, or 1% Club. We are required to always represent the fraternity in a positive light.

History of The North Wales Chapter.

Since the original talk that this book was created from was written as a lecture to be given primarily around the Province of North Wales, and as a founder member I have decided to include a brief history of the NWC.

In the summer of 2013, a few Freemasons from North Wales organised a three-day motorcycle tour of Wales to raise money for Combat Stress. A second three-day tour for charity was run in 2014.

These tours had two wondrous affects, firstly they raised over £30,000 for Charity, and secondly, they introduced the Widows Sons to North Wales, Thanks to members of several Chapters across the UK & Ireland taking part on the tours.

After talking to the Widows Sons on the tour, they suggested since we had enough Masonic Bikers to organise Charity Tours, we had enough to form a Widows Sons Chapter.

After discussions with The Provincial Grand Lodge of North Wales, and getting the OK from the both The United Grand Lodge, and the Provincial Grand Lodge, The North Wales Chapter was officially formed on Monday the 10th of November 2014 by nine founding members. We received our official Charter in July 2015 at the National Rally in London.

The Founder Members were: -

- Alan "Sully" Sullivan.
- Dave "Yosser" Hughes.
- Neville "Welsh Nev" Owens.
- Wayne "Pendragon" Owens.
- Keith "Major" Jarvis.
- Guy "Farmer" Jones.
- Graham "Ossie" Jones.
- Alan "Sat Nav" Doyle.
- Nick "Robbo" Roberts.

Since that date we have grown in strength, we now have over thirty members, and have brought many new candidates into Freemasonry.

We hosted the 2017 National Rally and Tercentenary Party in Mold which saw Masons from as far away as America, Canada and Germany attend.

We have also continued to raise money for various local charities.

Charity

As well as raising lots of money for various Charities, and to put another nail in the coffin of us being an Outlaw Gang, we also: -

Every Easter we organise Easter Egg runs. Which is where we collect Easter Eggs, toys, and Money and then ride out to give them to sick or disadvantaged Children in Hospitals, or Hostel's. The money pays for more toys for the children or is donated to the group looking after them. At Christmas we do Santa Runs which is the same idea, but often with people dressed up as Santa or elves.

Every year on the first Saturday of October, Widows Sons from all over the UK meet up to be part of the "Ride to The Wall", where several thousand motorcycles ride to the National Memorial Arboretum to pay respects to those who have dies in conflicts around the world. We then meet up in the Arboretum's Masonic Garden to pay our own Masonic respect.

During the Covid-Pandemic lockdown, a lot of the Widows Sons were out, helping their communities, delivering vital supplies, making PPE and delivering food parcels to those struggling as with many others who have jumped to help in the pandemic.

And thanks to the unusualness of a "Masonic Biker Gang", and the photogenic nature of big shiny motorcycles our charitable works are more likely to be featured in newspapers and shared over social media.

Blood Bikes.

> A BLOOD BIKE IS A MOTORCYCLE USED TO COURIER URGENT AND EMERGENCY MEDICAL ITEMS INCLUDING BLOOD, X-RAYS, SAMPLES, DRUGS, AND DOCUMENTATION BETWEEN HOSPITALS AND OTHER HEALTHCARE FACILITIES.

> IN THE UNITED KINGDOM AND IRELAND, A NETWORK OF INDEPENDENT REGISTERED CHARITIES, WHOSE MEMBERS ARE ALL UNPAID VOLUNTEERS, PROVIDE BLOOD BIKE COURIER SERVICES IN COLLABORATION WITH THEIR LOCAL HEALTHCARE AUTHORITIES

Most Widows Sons Chapters also have a strong connection with the various Blood Bikes Charities, with their members volunteering as riders, controllers, or members as well as raising money to support their running costs. It is also not unusual to find a square and compass somewhere on a Blood Bike.

The newly consecrated Widows Sons Lodge No. 10011 in combination with the Province of Yorkshire North & East Ridings donated a bike to Whiteknights Blood Bikes, as part of its consecration celebrations.

The North Wales Chapter has had three blood bike riders, and two controllers amongst its members,

The TLC.
Teddies for Loving Care

TEDDIES FOR LOVING CARE PROVIDES CUDDLY BEARS TO A&E DEPARTMENTS FOR MEDICAL STAFF TO GIVE TO YOUNG CHILDREN.

STAFF OFTEN USES THE BEARS TO CALM CHILDREN DOWN, REWARD THEM FOR BEING BRAVE, AND — IN SOME CASES — DEMONSTRATE PROCEDURES. THE TLC TEDDY HAS BECOME A USEFUL TOOL FOR MEDICAL PROFESSIONALS AND A REAL COMFORT FOR CHILDREN.

ESTABLISHED BY ESSEX FREEMASONS IN 2001, TLC IS NOW A NATIONAL PROGRAMME, LOCALLY LED BY FREEMASONS ACROSS ENGLAND AND WALES. SUPPORT AND ENTHUSIASM FOR THE INITIATIVE CONTINUES TO GROW, WITH MORE THAN 3.5 MILLION TEDDIES DISTRIBUTED NATIONWIDE TO OVER 250 HOSPITALS.

The final nail in the coffin of the Widows Sons being a bunch of rough and tough outlaw bikers are Teddy Bears, or TLC Teddies in particular.

At the beginning of May 2018, the Northumberland Chapter of the Widows Sons "adopted" two TLC bears, which they decided were a father and son named "Hiram" and "Biff".

Hiram was given, his own Cut, helmet, and was patched in as an honorary member of the Widows Sons. He travels on the back of a bike on all the Northumberland Chapter's runs, attends their events, and has even gone along with them to meetings at Grand Lodge. He is a huge hit with Children wherever they go, has popped up in several positive press articles, and has his own Social Media accounts, where he does a wonderful job of promoting the TLC, the Widows Sons, and Freemasonry in General.

Due to the Success Northumberland have had with Hiram, several other Widows Sons Chapters are looking into adopting TLC Bears and making them honorary members.

For those of you wondering, they must be honorary members because unlike Sooty, they will not have been raised to the degree of a Master Mason, which is a requisite for full membership of the Widows Sons.

If you were not aware; Brother Sooty was, Initiated, Passed, and Raised in Chevin Lodge No 6848, Where he took part fully in the ceremonies, but being both shy and cautious he answered all his questions in a whisper in Brother Harry Corbett's ear.

BRO. HARRY CORBETT, O.B.E.
1918 – 1989

So, who are the Widows Sons?

They are quite simply an internationally based motorcycle-riding club. They are non-brand specific, so no matter what brand of motorcycle you ride, if you are a Master Mason in good standing, you are welcome as a member.

Several Chapters have Associate-Membership for none-riding Brethren, and also have a Bad Pennies group open to none Masons, which helps to introduce Freemasonry to prospective new members.

They serve as a "Masonic Booster Club" by helping to raise Masonic Awareness while attending public events and rallies.

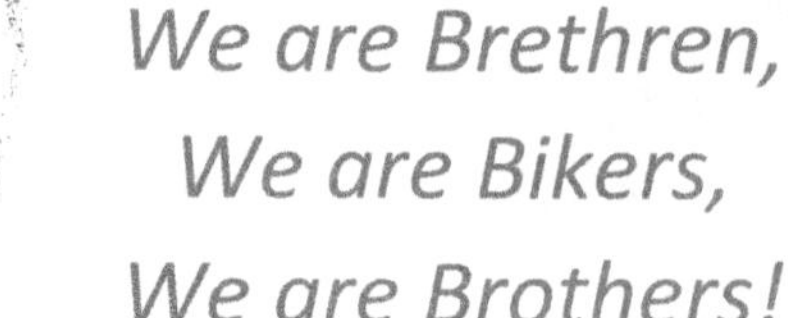

Hopefully, I have explained a little bit about how the Widows Sons help promote Freemasonry, the excellent work we do, and have convinced you all that we are more Masonic Ambassadors than Outlaw Bikers.

But for any of you still on the fence, I will point out we do have members who will not take their bike out if it is wet, or cold, or raining, or even if there is the slightest possibility of rain.

30

So here's to the sons of the widow,

Wherever soever they roam,

Here's to all they aspire,

And if they desire,

A speedy return to their home.

About the Author.

Wayne "Pendragon" Owens was born and raised in the mountains of North Wales. After school he trained to become an Electrician, a career he gave up after gaining his Degree in Electrical & Electronic Engineering to become an IT specialist working for an ISP.

He is a Past Master of several Lodges in the Province of North Wales, as well as a lecturer for the North Wales Association of Masonic Study (NWAMS).

He is a founder member of the North Wales Chapter of the Widows Sons MBA, and a controller/fundraiser for Blood Bikes Wales.

33